gADGETS and gIFTS

for GIRLS to MAKE

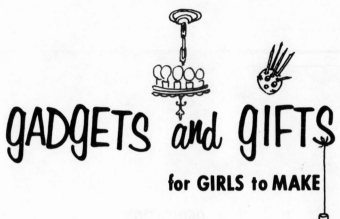

GADGETS and GIFTS

for GIRLS to MAKE

written and illustrated
by **SHEILA OSTRANDER**

GRAMERCY PUBLISHING COMPANY
New York

DEDICATION

For My Family

ACKNOWLEDGMENT

The author is indebted to the magazine *Calling All Girls* for permission to use much of the material appearing in this book, and also to *Teen-Agers Ingenue* for portions of "The Well-Groomed Desk."

CONTENTS

INTRODUCTION

This book supplies the keynotes to help you compose your own impromptu presents and projects. Whether you are harmonizing your room décor, arranging fashion accessories or conducting parties—here are scores of practical ideas which are shortcuts that will save you time and money in solving home and school problems, as well as whimsical novelties.

Both teen-leaders and teen-agers will find these versatile numbers are exceptionally givable gifts. Whether you work solo (and whip up a gift or two while babysitting), or in a chorus (as a special project), here are creative ways to add sparkling grace notes to your premises and have fun doing it. Besides, many of these confections lend themselves to encore performances at bazaars and fair booths to raise money for your club or charity.

From expensive boutique-inspired creations to household hints, the whole album of items can be made at virtually no cost simply by transposing scraps and discards into new settings or giving old objects new interpretations. Most of the materials involved can usually be found around the house or apartment although being a scavenger would have some advantages.

No special skills or tools are required . . . just originality. The instructions suggest only one of many possible ways to approach the subject. With a little imagination you will easily improvise your own variations on these themes.

CHAPTER I

CLOTHES CO-ORDINATES

A whole phrasebook of clothes co-ordinates to translate into conversation pieces for your wardrobe.

"SEE-WORTHY" BELT

Ship ahoy with a singular "see-worthy" belt. Make this nautical waist-cincher from a length of white rope long enough to go around your waist twice. Double the rope and tack it together with loops at intervals of a few inches. Stitch a buckle to one end of the belt and a short piece of leather to the other end. Punch a few holes in the leather piece to buckle it and you're all ready to unfurl your sails.

GLOVE TREE

It's gloverly, this glove-bearing tree in autumn colors that transforms a handsome piece of driftwood into an elegant accessory for your room. Gild the driftwood, glue it firmly to a mirror base, and it will be a genuine conversation piece. Gloves suspended gracefully from the branches are easy to co-ordinate with your daily wardrobe.

BELT HANGER

Belts in the plural suspend neatly and unwrinkled on a belt hanger. Screw cup hooks into the underside of a wooden hanger. Belts will wear longer if they're hung up instead of rolled up when not in use.

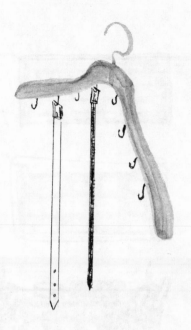

HAT HOLDER

Convert a carton into a high-up haven for hats. Cut off the top flaps and cut a large "V" in the back so that it will hinge up at the wide part. Cut a small hole in the "V" to serve as a hanger. Paint the box or cover it with wallpaper, insert your hat and hang it on a closet hook.

1.

2.

3.

Pluperfect purse arranger is made by measuring your purse and cutting a square of material (old tablecloth or remnant) the same width and double the height. Fold over and stitch at both ends. Push each end in about an inch so that it forms two tubular pockets, and stitch down on the outside. These four pockets hold pen, lipstick, nail file and pencil. The large space in the middle is reserved for wallet and keys. Add pockets for more paraphernalia if needed. This bundle of pockets is ideal for organizing purse contents or making quick changeovers from one purse to another.

HANDBAG HOLDER

Conjugate purses in a handbag holder. To a long piece of cardboard about a foot wide attach several large transparent plastic bags. Attach them sideways on the board so that the opening is on the right. Purses will slip in easily, stay dustless and ready for use, and you'll save valuable shelf space.

PETTICOAT DRYER

A petticoat dryer to keep your crinoline in A-1 shape after it's been washed and starched. Hang it over an open umbrella. The dampness of the petticoat won't affect the umbrella and the crinoline will dry in exactly the shape you want it.

SHIRTTAIL TUCKER

No more will blouses and/or shirttails make unexpected appearances if you wear a shirttail tucker. Cut a belt of material long enough to go around you about an inch below your waist. Stitch elastic bands every which way along the length of the belt. Add hooks and eyes and wear it low slung on top of your blouse, inside shirts or slacks. No matter how athletic your day, your shirttail won't be hanging out.

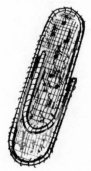

LINGERIE CLASPS

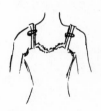

If your lingerie straps seem to have culti- vated the habit of constantly slipping off your shoulders, these smart lingerie clasps may be first-aid. You can make top-rate strap aligners from fairly large paperclips. Sew a tiny piece of cloth to each side of the clip and stitch beads or rhinestones to the cloth. Clasp a clutch of straps at each shoulder.

Let your rubbers match your coat and keep high-water marks off your stockings to boot. Cut two pieces of coat material 4 inches wide and as long as the distance around the top of your boots plus an inch. Stitch the ends of each piece together to form two circles of cloth. Slip them over the tops of your boots and fold inside about 2 inches. Tack the boot shields in place with thread.

BOOT SHIELDS

FOOT NOTES

No need to throw away a good pair of shoes because the insole linings are torn. For sure footing, cut another lining from cardboard, but before gluing it in place, cover it with a foot cut from an old pair of nylons. The nylon covering keeps your feet from sticking to the lining and prevents the cardboard from ripping.

TWINKLE TOES

Replace a lost shoe buckle or make your shoes unique and chic with a puff of fur in place of a shoe ornament. Choose a color of fur to match or contrast with your shoes, then glue or stitch a small dot of fur to the top of each shoe.

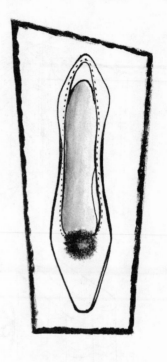

PADABOUTS

Padabouts to be glad about are these lighthearted circus slippers. Trace the pattern of your feet onto pieces of foam plastic, then cut out the soles of your slippers. Cut out two more pieces slightly wider and shorter for the tops. From contrasting plastic or cloth cut out mouth, eyes and eyebrows, and stitch to the slipper tops. Embroider on a nose, stitch the tops to the soles and your slippers are ready to clown around in.

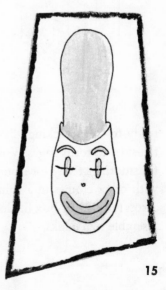

15

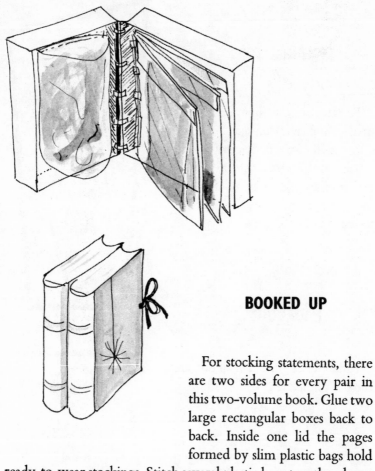

BOOKED UP

For stocking statements, there are two sides for every pair in this two-volume book. Glue two large rectangular boxes back to back. Inside one lid the pages formed by slim plastic bags hold ready-to-wear stockings. Stitch several plastic bags together down the sides to form pages. Volume II contains one large plastic bag for stockings ready for laundry, safe from runs they might collect with other clothes in a laundry bag. Stitch the large plastic bag across the back of Box II. Cover the boxes with wrapping paper to resemble two books.

HOSE DRYER

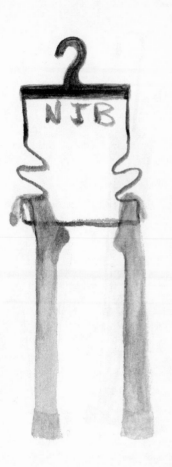

No more mix-ups with Mother or Sister over whose hose is whose with this handy hose dryer of your own. Cut a square of cardboard $5\frac{1}{2}''$ x $5\frac{1}{2}''$. Cut two V-shaped slits on each side. Coat the slits with clear nail polish to avoid any sharp edges that might pick your stockings. Staple onto the top a piece of cardboard shaped like a hanger. Paint on your initials. Make some for Mom and Sis too.

UMBRELLEGANT

For your umbrella use a man's tie to keep it dustless. Find one of Dad's or Brother's discarded ties. Slip your umbrella into the tie at the large end and clip the tie off to the correct length at the small end. For that added touch and to keep the clipped end from fraying, stitch a length of ribbon around it and add a bow.

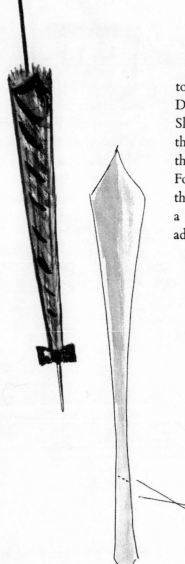

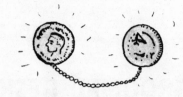

SWEATER
LINKS

Sweater Links are bright accents for cardigans worn capelike over your shoulders. Glue two small safety clasps or safety pins to the back of two shiny new pennies or two foreign coins. Attach one coin to each end of a discarded locket or key chain and link up a sweater.

SWEATER DRYER

If your family and pets seem to have a curious habit of managing to step on your sweaters while they're drying, avoid leap-frogging problems and keep the floor free with a sweater dryer. Cover a large piece of cardboard with oilcloth or plastic. Place two extra long lengths of string diagonally across the cardboard and stitch them firmly to each corner. Attach a hook and your sweaters can be hung up to dry on a clothesline or shower rod.

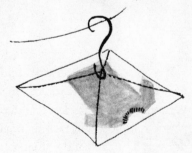

CHAPTER 2

THE WELL-GROOMED DESK

Add desk appeal to homework quarters with a cast of lighthearted desk workers. Spotlight or chorus rôle, they give a sparkling performance.

DRAWER POCKETS

If you're concerned with undercover operatives, be on your toes for opening scenes when it comes to drawers with these versatile drawer pockets. Cut off the toe section of worn-out plastic rainshoes and tack them along the inside edges of the desk drawer. They're handy holders for desk flotsam.

WALL NOOK

Clear working space on your desk by keeping tabs on desk overflow with a decorative wall nook. Suspend an enormous cloth tab from your bulletin board and button it to a slim box. When your desk is snowed under, you'll welcome this extra drawer.

PEN

FEATHER

Feather your desk nest with a plumed holder for ballpoint pen or pencil. Turn a funnel upside down and glue a swoop of feather to the pointed section. Paint the funnel attractively or cover with silver or gold gift paper and install on your desk as a unique pen-holder.

MAP
HOLDER

Two slices of a car or bicycle tire casing tacked under your desk top will hold rolled art work, projects or maps safely out of the way.

HAND PAPERWEIGHT

You'll get a "big hand" for your memos when you transform an old glove. Insert cardboard, cut to fit, to hold the shape. Fill the thumb with heavy nails, stitch it across the base, and this practical paperweight will keep mail and notes always under your thumb.

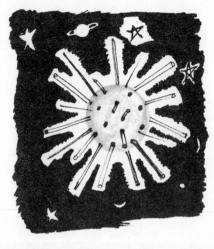

PENCIL STAR

Special sputnik for your pencils keeps an array of writing and drawing supplies glittering at your fingertips. Bore numerous holes all over an old sponge ball and then paint the ball gold. Cut a flat area for the bottom. Insert pens and pencils point first in each of the holes and this new constellation will ornament your desk or shelf.

PENCIL FISHING

Be sure of a big catch when you're fishing for a pencil with this denizen of the deep. Cut a flat edge on one side of an old sponge ball. In a circle around the top cut several holes large enough to hold pencils. Paint on a fish face and glue on a sturdy cardboard tail to serve as a rudder. Sit him on your desk and fill to the gills with pencils.

THE DESK PICTURESQUE

Sweet notes with a golden horn. Writing notes is easier when pens and pencils stand at attention. Paint an old toy horn gold, glue it to a wooden base and install pens, brushes, and pencils. The horn handle takes care of memos.

PENCIL RECORD

For the record, harmonize your writing supplies on a disc of recorded music. Heat an old record till pliable and bend it to form a trough. Glue slices of eraser to the bottom to stabilize the holder.

POCKET PENCIL

A giant pencil to pocket miscellaneous items from a VIP desk. Cut a long sliver of heavy cloth in the shape of a pencil, stitch on envelope pockets every few inches and paint on a fresh-from-the-pencil-sharpener point. Hang on your wall and organize desk supplies such as pens, pencils, notes and letters.

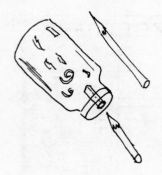

PENCIL

SHARPENER

Save yourself the trouble of having to run to a wastebasket every time you sharpen a pencil with this handy pencil-shaving-holder. Remove the lid from a glass jar and punch a hole in it large enough for a pencil to go through. With household cement, carefully glue your pencil sharpener over the hole in the lid so that it will be on the inside of the jar. Screw the lid on the jar and it's ready for sharpening.

SEE-THROUGH

PENCIL BOX

A nifty pen and pencil box that reminds you what to put in it can be made from a toothbrush container. With nail polish write little reminders to yourself all over the container such as "eraser", "pencil", "refills", etc. Because you can see inside this pencil box, you're less likely to forget the items you've written on it.

KEYBOARD

For keys unconfused make a practical keyboard chart. Cut out a typewriter keyboard illustration and back it with cardboard. Attach keys belonging to different doors to the appropriate alphabet letter.

CRESTED TACKS

Escutcheons emblazoned with a coat-of-arms in tacks are always handy near your bulletin board or desk. Cut shields from bright felt for a note of elegance that will be felt.

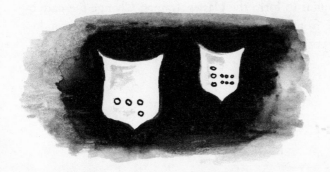

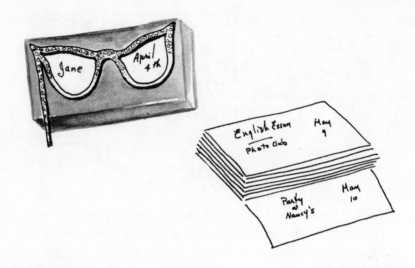

LONG-SIGHTED SPECTACLES

These bewitched spectacles will peer into your future to remind you of important dates. Clip numbers from an old calendar and paste them on the right-hand side of $3'' \times 5''$ cards. List on the left-hand side of the cards special occasions occurring on that date such as birthdays, assignments due, etc. Place the cards in order inside a box. Clip two windows in the box lid in the shape of lenses, and glue on sequins to form the glasses' frames. Change the date by moving the front card to the back. These specs never let you lose sight of important events.

DESK DASHBOARD

Dispense erasers and desk appointments from a desk dashboard. Halve a waxpaper tube, divide into compartments, glue on toothpaste tube caps to prevent rolling, paint, and then slide in supplies —stamps, clips, erasers, rubber bands, etc.

MINIATURE MATCHBOXES

Apply two-way tactics to stubborn small items with a set of miniature matchboxes glued end to end. A push at either end and a matchless row of supplies is at your fingertips, clearly classified into compartments.

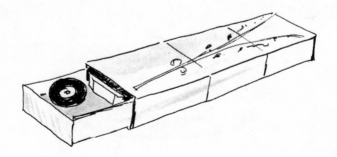

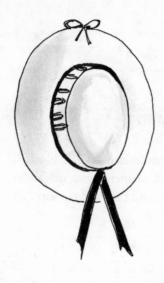

HAT HOLDER

If desk litter just seems too utterly chaotic for you, keep it under your hat—an old, fairly large, stiff-crowned one. Hinge the hat-brim to a large circle of cardboard. Stitch cloth pockets to the cardboard to hold stapler, scissors, tape, rulers, pens, etc. The hatband holds clips, pins and erasers. Hang the hat upon the wall or leave it on the desk—and yours will be the best-dressed desk in the house.

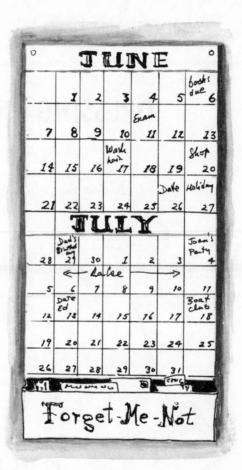

FORGET-ME-NOT

For distant perspectives, keep clued in with an over-all view of several months at a time. Cut six large sheets of paper, either white or brown. Rule seven spaces across and eight or nine down, leaving an extra bit of paper at the bottom to fold up into a pocket. Cut up a small regular calendar and glue a number into each square, two months per page. Hang the calendar near the phone. There's lots of room in each square to jot down red-letter days.

CHAPTER 3

DRESSING-TABLE TIPS

For the gifted giver a mine of purse-pleasing gift ideas that won't send a budget off the gold standard. Or make them as a present for yourself.

TO THE POINT

From the Wizard of Oz perhaps, a medium-sized oil tin gilded and garnished with shell flowers to grace a special dressing table. Fill this unique ornament with hand lotion and it's always ready to dispense just the right number of drops without mess or spill.

SPILL-PROOF CASE

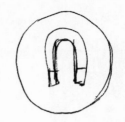

No more hours spent picking up a boxful of spilled bobby pins. Glue a small magnet to the bottom of a typewriter ribbon tin. Clip off the rubber tip from a mucilage bottle and glue it to the lid of the tin as a handy opener for the bobby pins. Paint the outside and fill with pins. Even if your bobby-pin holder should tip over, the pins won't spill out.

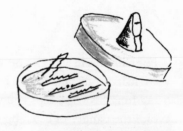

CLIP CLARA

Pamper yourself with a 'tween-time hairclip holder. Clips are easy to get hold of without chipping fingernails wrestling them out of a box. Cut out a large oval face (about 7" in diameter) from heavy corrugated cardboard. Paint features on the lower half of the circle. Over all the top part stitch on medium-sized wool pincurls. When you're not using your hairclips, clip one to each of the woolly curls. Your holder can be hung on the wall or lie flat on your dresser.

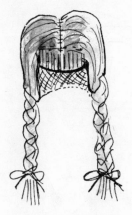

WIG WARM

For hairclips in action, you won't get caught unexpectedly with your hair up in pins if you're wearing a "wacky" wig. Besides being fun, this wig keeps you warm while pincurls are drying and avoids the danger of catching cold. Make it from a hairnet elasticized around the edge. Loop several swatches of wool or angel's hair into curls or pigtails complete with bangs, and stitch a seam down the middle to form a part. Stitch the wool to the hairnet and the wig pulls on easily to keep pincurls undercover.

RIBBON BAR

Keep a gathering of ribbons and headbands unwrinkled and un-crunched. Hang them on this non-slip ribbon bar. Wrap a strip of velvet ribbon or cloth along the length of a towel rack and screw the rack to the back of a closet door. Even slippery ribbons stay put in easy-to-choose order on this velvet rack.

34

PIN-UP
FOR
PINS

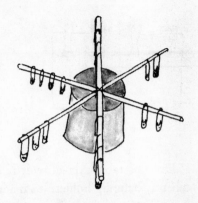

"Star" billing for safety pins is a pin-up made by cutting shallow notches every $\frac{1}{4}''$ along the length of three straws and then cutting each straw in half. Glue one end of each of the halves to the middle of the bottom of a cutdown paper cup in order to form a star. Paint the holder with poster paints. When it's dry, hang safety pins in the notches where they'll always be handy.

EMERY-BOARD STAR

Playing a leading rôle is this star emery-board holder. Wrap a piece of velvet around a $4''$ square of cardboard and stitch it firmly underneath. Choose several of your brother's prettiest marbles and glue them in a small circle on the velvet. Nail files, emery boards, and manicure items slide easily into place in between the marbles to form a star, and are always handy for quick nail repairs.

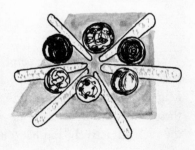

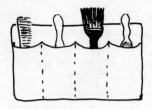

BRUSH HOLDER

Dressing table over-crowded? Keep your combs and brushes in a handy hanging holder. It's made from a piece of cloth 16″ × 14″. Fold up 6″ and stitch four pockets each 4 inches wide. Hang your brush holder on the wall with adhesive tape and insert brushes, combs and a mirror.

COMB RACK

Or file your combs in a comb rack. Cut several cardboard tubes (the kind that wax paper or paper towels are rolled on) in half lengthwise. Shorten them to the length of your combs and staple these cardboard holders $2\frac{1}{2}$″ apart on a square of cardboard. Paint the rack attractively and hang it near your dresser.

CHAPTER 4

HOBBIES

Put your best foot forward with these handy hobby helpers.

COIN TRAY

Add new appeal to an accumulation of coins or stamps by showing off the most unusual items on this smart serving tray or wall decoration made from a picture frame. Back a piece of dark felt or velvet cut to the size of the frame with heavy cardboard or light wood. Frame the velvet and glue on the coins or stamps.

TIRE GARDEN

New destination for an old tire is a flower garden for your room. Cut a section from an old tire casing, paint it and install plants in tins or pots. There's no danger of mess from spilled water or soil with such a leakproof holder and you can easily move the whole flower garden around to follow the sun.

HOBBY PICTURES

Spotlight your hobby collection and clever fabrications as part of your room décor. If you collect miniature dolls, for instance, frame your collection to hang up in your room. From plastic or

bamboo place-mats cut rectangles slightly larger than the doll. Staple or glue on a cardboard frame. Paint the frame and wire your doll firmly to the bamboo rectangle. Frame several of your dolls and arrange on your walls.

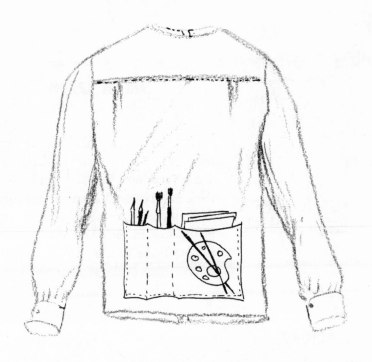

PAINTING SMOCK

Very palette-able, a professional-looking artist's smock to protect you from paint spots. Remove the collar from one of Dad's
or Brother's old shirts and turn the shirt front to back. Cut off the
shirttails and stitch them on the front of the smock as large
pockets. Stitch in sections for brushes, paints, rags, etc.

GARDEN APRON

For the gardening hobbyist cut out the front of an old pair of slacks or denims and lop off the legs just below the knees. Thread an apron tie through the loops at the waistband and stitch a plastic bag to each knee for sponge pads to make kneeling easier. Attach roomy patch-pockets for garden tools.

COLLECTOR'S CORNERS

Collections of all sorts, butterflies to rocks, go promptly portable in this attractive corner. Cut a rectangle of oil-cloth about 24″ wide by 20″ high. Fold a 4″ border on three sides. Flap the side sections over onto the bottom border to form shelf corners and stitch firmly into place. Install a flat piece of light wood 24″ × 4″ to make the shelf hold its shape. Lace the oilcloth tightly to the bottom edge of a wooden hanger. Taper the side sections from the corners to the top.

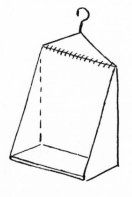

HOBBY
DRAWER

Your collections of buttons, shells, rocks, etc., won't get spilled and can be seen at a glance with a "hobby drawer". Slice wax-paper tubes into pieces as high as your drawer. Fill a whole drawer with these midget tubes and sort your collections into these exclusive circles.

SHELF AID
FOR SHY SHELVES

Turn retiring shelves into show-offs for your hobbies or ornaments. Eliminate deep shelf disappearances by installing a few bricks. Paint bricks to match your room and glue felt on the bottom to avoid scratching. Line up a row of bricks on edge at the back of the shelf, and another row in front lying flat. Set up the contents on your shelf, small items in front, larger things behind. All will be easily visible.

CHAPTER 5

JEWELRY

Don't hide away your jewelry. With a little wizardry and wit you can transform your room into a treasure-trove.

JEWEL COLLAR

Collar your necklaces in a unique jewel case. Use the collar of a discarded blouse or make one from a scrap of material. Stitch the collar around the outside edges to a rectangle of felt or velvet. Glue to a piece of cardboard and use as décor for your wall or dressing table. Drape your necklaces inside.

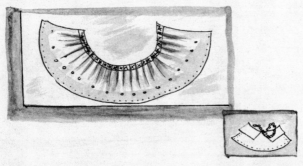

COLLAR
YOUR
ANIMALS

Tame a tangled jungle of stuffed animals with your bangles, baubles and bracelets. You can make your jewelry selection at jiffy-speed. The animal statues in their chic collars will be regal mascots for your room.

Distinctive and elegant setting for rings and bracelets is this golden bough. Gild a small branch of driftwood. Use household cement to glue the branch to a mirror or tray base. Cover the bottom of the mirror with felt to prevent scratching. Show off your necklaces, rings, beads and pendants on this glittering gadget.

GOLDEN
BOUGH

43

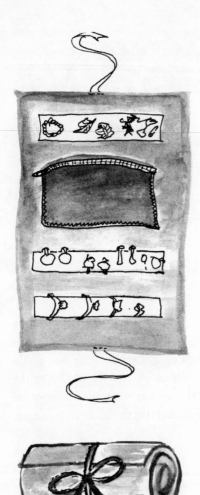

GEM ROLL

For gypsying jewelry why not make a gem roll? Cut a length of felt or velvet about 6″×9″. Sew on a rectangle of felt across the top for pinning in brooches. To hold necklaces and beads, find a small zipper purse or make one from velvet and stitch it to the jewel holder below the brooch section. Stitch on two more narrow strips of felt-covered cardboard below the purse for attaching earrings and rings. Roll up your jewel case, add ribbon ties and your jewelry is safe from scratches and loss, convenient to carry on trips.

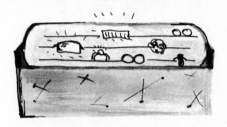

JEWEL NEST

Pick out the ring or pin you want to wear with a flick of your jewel twirler. Cut a short length from a wax-paper tube and glue a covering of velvet firmly around the tube. Cut slits through the velvet and the tube lengthwise at $\frac{1}{2}''$ intervals. Glue circles of cardboard at each end of the tube, and place it in a box. Insert a nail through each end of the box into the ends of the tube so that it can turn. Insert cuff links, rings, earrings and pins for a beady-eyed jewel selector.

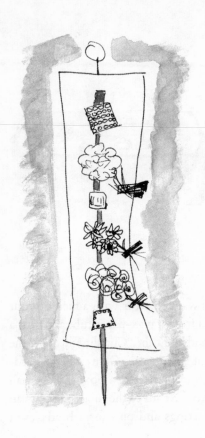

FLORAL PIN-UPS

Try a streamer for your jewelry and artificial flowers on a free-form strip of material pinned to wall or bulletin board. Attach flowers to this backdrop with colored plastic clothespins.

BRACELET BAR

When not being worn, your watch is in safe "arms" installed on this bracelet bar along with a wristful of jewelry. Glue a velvet-sheathed cardboard tube to a square of wood painted brightly and sprinkled with gold dust.

SCATTERED SCATTER PINS

Make a splendiferous storehouse for scatter pins. Tack up large swatches of black felt to your bedroom wall and spatter with scatter pins, brooches, clips, etc. Safekeeps pins from the wear and tear of a jewel box, and it's black-magic for a wall.

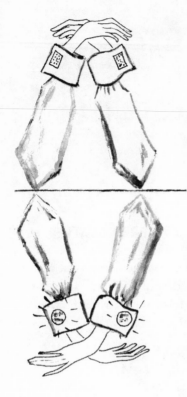

"DATED"
CUFF LINKS

Mark red-letter days in your life with "dated" cuff links. Cut from a tiny plastic calendar several special months of the year for you—i.e. yours or friends' birthdays, special celebrations, etc. Circle the day to be remembered. Find several fair-size square buttons and loop to each one a smaller button in order to form links. Glue a different calendar month to each of the large square buttons, and vary the pair as you fancy.

BUTTON MUSIC

Music is always at your fingertips with these musical cuff links. Find two large flat white buttons that are smooth on top. Using India ink, draw music staffs on the buttons and trace a few notes at random or a song. With heavy thread link each button to another smaller button to form a cuff link.

EYEGLASS
BROOCH

Hang unused glasses on a convenient brooch that keeps them safe from breakage and leaves your hands free. Make a small loop out of $\frac{1}{2}''$-wide elastic and slide it over the pin at the back of a fairly large brooch. Attach the brooch to your dress and slip the earpiece of the glasses through the elastic loop on the pin.

PURSE WHISK

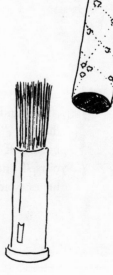

A pixie-size purse whisk is a handy helper for purse, pocket or home base. Carefully remove all the lipstick from a large empty lipstick tube. From an old broom cut a clump of straw about $1\frac{1}{2}''$ long. Fill the lipstick holder with household cement and insert the clump of bristles. Hold them in place until the cement sets.

SCREWY
CUFF LINKS

Lost one of your best cuff links? Try these "screwy" endings for sleeves. Find two screws about a half-inch long with large flat heads. If they're too long you can file them down. Paint the screw top with nail polish to cover sharp edges. When they're dry, slip them through your cuffs and attach nuts painted the same color.

PICTURE
LINKS

You and your best friend will be officially "linked" with these perky photo cuff links. Cut a tiny photo of yourself and your friend and carefully glue one picture to each cuff link.

CHAPTER 6

KITCHEN WIRES

For good connections in the kitchen, try some of these tickets.

**A
TICK-TACK
CLOCK**

You'll always have a tack in time with this unique tack holder—a glittering felt clock. It's made from a circle of felt 7″ or 8″ in diameter. Glue on silver paper numerals and tack in two cardboard hands. All around the edge goes your supply of tacks. The hands of the clock may be turned to remind you of the time of special engagements or meetings.

PANELED
APRON

Make an apron with built-in hand wipers. Remove the waistband from an apron and stitch an attractive hand towel along the waistline on each side. Sew the waistband back on again. The towels, in addition to being useful, form smart-looking floating panels.

DRINK
SERVER

Piloting soft drinks to serve your friends won't give you spill-itis with this beverage server. Dress up an old muffin tin with a bright coat of paint and a few decals. Fill your glasses and insert one into each space. Glasses can't move around, won't spill.

EAT YOUR PARTY DISHES

If dishwashing takes the fizz out of festivities you can save Mom and yourself extra work by serving party desserts, such as custards or gelatin treats, in the cones used for ice cream. Your guests will love your unusual dessert and you won't have to waste time doing dishes afterwards.

BROWNIE DECORATOR

Your chocolate brownies (or other cookies) will take the prize when they're patterned with a contemporary design. Fold up a piece of wax paper into eights, snip out pieces here and there to form a design, open it out and spread it over your brownies while they're still in the pan. Sprinkle icing sugar over the pattern, lift off and presto! —your brownies have an elaborate design etched in white.

CHAPTER 7

LETTER HOLDERS

A whole alphabet of red-letter ideas for your better letters.

LETTERED
WHALE

A whale of a dish and the biggest catch for correspondence is this "lettered" whale. He's actually a large rubber or sponge ball transformed. Cut 6 or 8 slices evenly about half through, paint on features and add a glittery paper tail and nose. Bait with letters and notes.

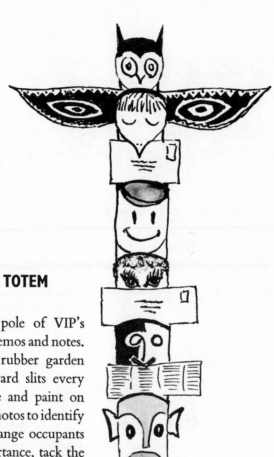

LETTER TOTEM

A tall totem pole of VIP's handles letters, memos and notes. On a length of rubber garden hose cut downward slits every $1\frac{1}{2}''$ or so. Carve and paint on faces or glue on photos to identify each section. Arrange occupants in order of importance, tack the totem pole on your bulletin board or wall and these worthies will put the bite on papers and letters according to what must be done first.

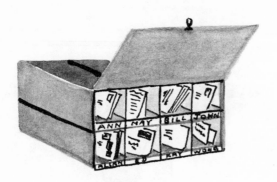

PIGEON HOLES

Pen pal perfect is a set of pigeon holes to file your correspondence. Cut off the tops from several milk cartons and glue the cartons together side by side. Cut a rectangular piece of cardboard to fit the front and tape it along the top of the cartons to flap down as a cover. Fasten with a loop and a button. Label compartments alphabetically with pen pals' names and file your letters in the proper pigeon hole.

LETTER COMB

Comb through your mail in minutes with correspondence combs. In a piece of corrugated cardboard 5" × 9" cut two grooves about 3 inches apart and with household cement glue a comb into each slit. Paint the holder and its multi-teeth are ready to untangle postcards and letters.

CHAPTER 8

FOR MAGAZINES AND BOOKS

*Due respect for the printed page will lead
you unerringly to adopt many of these ideas.*

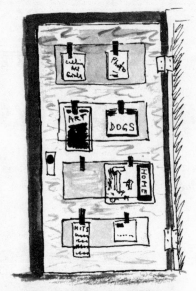

DOOR RACK

For shuffle-free viewing, frame your magazines on a clothespin rack. Screw a few spring clothespins, snap-end down, across the back of your closet door, two to each panel. Simply insert magazines in the clothespins for an attractive space-saving arrangement.

PORTABLE MAGAZINE RACK

A travelling exposition is this magazine and book rack that can follow you wherever you go. Press down the bottom rung of a wire coathanger and pull it out lengthwise. Then bend the bottom of the hanger into an upward curve. Fill the rack with magazines or books and you can hang it beside you in the car, on your deskchair, or on a doorknob in your room.

58

3-IN-1 BOOK COVER

Have designs on your book covers to help eyeglasses stick close to the book. Cut a piece of felt 5″×3″ and glue to it two round black eyes. Cut a piece of red felt about 2½″ square in the shape of a mouth. Stitch it to the specs holder around the outside edge of the mouth so that it forms a pocket. Insert a package of spectacle polishers and tape these 3-in-1 holders to the covers of your most often used books.

WELL-DRESSED BOOK BASKET

A double-duty wastebasket warmly sweatered in a discarded V-necked pullover holds magazines and books as well as scraps. Tack the sweater in place down the sides and underneath the basket, then fill the pockets thus formed with your current reading matter. A sweater-basket warms to the subject. It becomes not only a space-saver but a scene-stealer.

59

CAT TALES

These two librarian cats have many a tale to their tails. Pussyfoot bookends are made from two fairly large, flat metal angle-brackets. Cut two cat's faces from cardboard, glue one to each bracket and paint them both black. Books are supported by sitting on the long flat part of the bracket.

BOOK ANGLES

A big draw for books—a stacked rack. Cut a length of heavy wood about $16'' \times 6\frac{1}{2}''$. To the bottom of one end nail or glue a block of wood about $1''$ high. To the top of the other end attach a piece of wood about $6\frac{1}{2}'' \times 4''$, then paint the rack. To make it sturdier, brace the upright piece with one or two slim angle brackets.

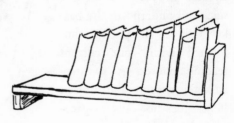

BOOKWORM
BOOKMARKS

Bookworm bookmarks for even a gallery of books are made in a matter of minutes. Simply cut off the corner of an envelope. From contrasting paper cut out a wiggly worm and draw on eyes and a mouth with India ink. Glue it angleways across the envelope corner. You can make many of these bookworm bookmarks for your friends too.

PET GUARD

Harness up your pet toy animals and let them guard the page between reading sessions. Braid a leash for each of them from strips of crepe paper. Attach the leash around the toy dog's neck, then slip it across a page of your book. Close the book and let your toy take charge seated on top of the cover.

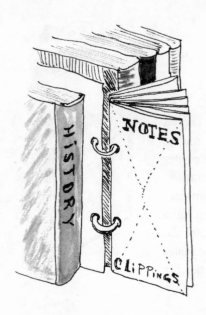

REVOLVING FILE

Of initial importance, an alphabetical file for notes and clippings. Stamps, labels, pictures, etc., are also at your fingertips in this revolving file. Seal about a half dozen old envelopes, then stand them on end and slit open the top of each one. Label each envelope. Punch two holes 5″ apart on the side of each envelope. Punch corresponding holes in a slightly larger rectangle of heavy cardboard. Insert two metal rings from a discarded looseleaf binder and slide the cardboard between books on your desk or bookshelf for handy reference.

CHAPTER 9

PARTY PERKERS

*Get into the spirit of enter-
taining with a batch of
bright ideas.*

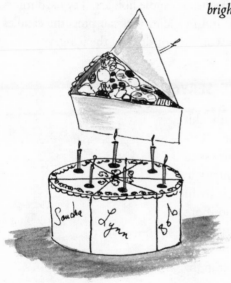

GIANT

PARTY CAKE

An entertaining idea to invite to your next party is a giant party cake you can eat and still have. It's made of cardboard. Cut two circles of cardboard about 14″ in diameter and cut each circle into six wedges. Cut cardboard ends and sides to fit each wedge and tape together on the inside, leaving one side of the top open so that it will lift up. Put the six wedges together to form the cake and decorate. Fill the wedges with candy, cake and favors and top off with candles.

CANDLE
CANDIES

If party cake candles have a tendency to droop over and drip wax onto your cake, use candies as candle holders. Try hard mints with built-in holes or soft gum candies you can press the candles into. Candles held firmly won't tip or drip on the icing.

SODA-BOTTLE COOKIE SERVER

Surprise the tribe with this cookie server made of three TV-dinner trays and a king-size soda bottle. Cut circular openings in each tray just big enough to fit snugly at the indicated positions on the bottle. With adhesive tape attach the first one firmly a bit below the top, the next in the middle and the third near the bottom. Brighten the server with painted designs and top it off with streamers stuck in a cork inserted in the bottle.

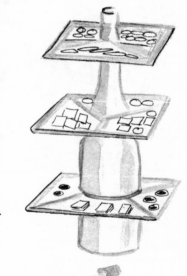

RARE BIRD JOCKEY

It's an instant party when this rare bird—a soda jockey—descends on your back yard. Nail two 4″ sticks of sturdy wood to the bottom of a muffin tin to form the bird's legs. Nail the feet to a flat square wooden base about 5″ × 5″. Tape on a long pipe-cleaner neck. A small ball forms the head. Draw on features and add a cardboard beak. Tape loops to each side of the tin for paper napkins which serve temporarily, as the bird's wings. Fan-fold a square of paper and tape it to the back end of the tin, inserting bright straws for the bird's tail feathers. Paint your bird, load him up with soft drinks and invite him to your next soda-pop and cookie session.

LAP DECK

Buffet and barbecue dinners won't become juggling matches for your guests if you equip each person with a handy lap deck. First cover a piece of heavy cardboard 14″ × 10″ with plastic cloth from an old shower curtain. Cut another piece of plastic 10″ × 15″. Fold up 7″ and stitch pockets $1\frac{1}{2}$″ wide for napkins, spoon, knife and fork, and a 4″ pocket for a glass. Stitch the pocket section to the side of the tray and your lap deck is ready to keep you lap-happy.

SNACK MAPS

Out-of-this-world snack maps will help locate your next party. Make them from $11\frac{1}{4}$″ × $17\frac{1}{2}$″ sections cut from a map of your area (obtainable from a local service station), or any part of the world, cemented to cardboard. Glue on a small pocket to hold a napkin. Spray with shellac and edge with strips of black paper.

BOTTLE BIBS

With these perky bottle covers you won't arrive at the picnic without the bottle openers and there will be no more spills due to slippery bottles. Cut a piece of cloth in the shape of an apron about $3'' \times 5''$. Add a neck strap and ties. Stitch on a tiny pocket $2'' \times 1\frac{1}{2}''$ to hold the bottle opener. Tie bottle bibs on all your soft drinks. They'll be a hit at your next celebration.

NUTTY SODA STIRRERS

Make nutty soda stirrers to match-mate with your friends! Stick peanut shells on the tops of long plastic drink stirrers. Paint on grinning faces with poster paint and add funny hats made of a twist of paper. They're sure to stir up a lot of talk at any group session.

CRACKER BARREL

A clever conversation piece for parties or jam-sessions is a genuine cracker barrel made from a circular cardboard carton. Arrange several crackers, cookies or potato chips in the form of flowers and glue them in place. Paint on stems and leaves and then varnish the holder.

CHAPTER 10

FOR THE PET SET

Stroke your pets the right way and at the same time make your own life simpler with these doggy ideas.

IDENTIFIER

For a regular full-time rover, there's little danger of getting lost when a pooch or pussy wears a lipstick-tube identity case. Punch a hole at each end of the empty lipstick tube and thread it onto a collar of ribbon or leather. Place inside the tube a card bearing your dog's or cat's vital statistics.

DOG WRAP

In wet weather, wrap your pooch in a personalized dog wrap. Cut a rectangle of plastic (to reach from his tail to his chest) from an old raincoat or plastic tablecloth. At one end cut out an oval for his head and sew on a snap-fastener. Stitch a strip of cloth long enough to go around your dog's middle across the rectangle and attach hooks to the ends. Personalize the wrap with his name and stitch on a tiny map of your district with your house circled. Should he ever get lost, you're sure of his speedy return.

A chow mat keeps your dog's food off the floor and saves you the trouble of cleaning up after your pet eats. Cut a large circle of cardboard about 12″ in diameter and cover it with oilcloth. Cut a one-inch strip of cardboard long enough to fit around your dog's dish and glue this strip in a circle in the middle of the chow mat.

CHOW MAT

PUSS IN BOOTS

Your puss or pup will spend less time in the doghouse drying off when he can foot it dryly in these practical pet rubbers. Make them by stitching ribbon ties to four small bags made of heavy plastic. On rainy or snowy days your pet will put his best foot forward in these attractive booties.

PUT ON THE DOG

You never have to hunt for your dog's things when he has his own dog caddy on a wall or closet door. Cut a fairly large rectangle of cardboard and tack onto it pockets of heavy cloth for your dog's collar, leash, comb and other belongings. Personalize it with your dog's signature by dipping his paw in ink and pressing it onto the cardboard.

PORTABLE PETS

Make this handy pet carrier from a discarded airline bag. Cut windows for ventilation on the front and sides of the bag and stitch pieces of screen over them. Remove the zipper from the bag to make it easy for your pet to get in and out of the carrier. At the front stitch on two triangular flaps of matching material to help keep him warm. A carrier is ideal for car-travelling pets because it keeps their fur off the upholstery.

CHAPTER 11

PHOTO FUN

Here are a phew phunny ideas for photo phun.

BULB TOTER

This uncrushable flashbulb toter is ready for take-off with any camera girl. Cut off a section of an egg carton consisting of from four to six compartments. Cut four narrow slits in the back side of the box and thread a belt through them. Keep it closed with reusable gummed tape. Paint the toter and fill it with bulbs. Belt it around your waist and you have flashbulbs at your fingertips.

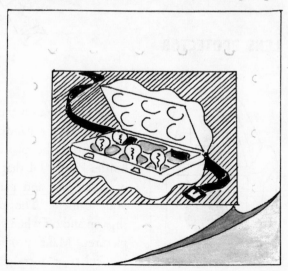

A photo whirl turns snapshots into "motion" pictures with a flick of the finger. Place two small tin pie plates back to back and attach with a nail through the middle. Cover all sharp edges with adhesive tape. Cut a length of broomstick and cut slits in it lengthwise $\frac{1}{4}''$ apart. Glue the broomstick to the tin plates, paint it and insert snapshots in each slot. All your prized photos are visible with a twirl of the holder.

PHOTO WHIRL

LENS PROTECTOR

For a camera on the move, protect the lens with a handy lens protector made from the plastic lid of a pill bottle. Find a lid that will fit snugly over the lens and paint it to match your camera. The protector easily slips on and off when you want to take pictures. Make protectors for your binoculars or opera glasses as well.

FAN TALE

Orbiting in the right circles
are these photo pins of your best
friends. Ask your pals for photos
of themselves. Cut out a silhou-
ette and trace it on two pieces of
medium-weight cardboard. Cut
out and glue the cardboard
shapes together for backing, and
glue on the photo. Tape a safety
pin on the back.

PHOTO PINS

Try a Fan Tale for all your
fans and friends. Cut several thin
strips of paper about $\frac{1}{2}'' \times 2\frac{1}{2}''$.
On each strip draw or glue an
attractive design. Pile the strips
on top of each other and put a
pin through them at the bottom.
To the top of each strip in the
fan, glue a tiny photo of a friend.
For added flair attach your Fan
Tale to your dress with a brooch.

PHOTO STAND

All you need for a special antenna-shaped stand for a prized photo is a pair of bobby pins. Use rubber-tipped pins to avoid scratches. Bend the back part of the pins downward to form a support and insert the pictures between the prongs. Paint the pins to match the color scheme in your room.

TURN-UP PHOTO ALBUM

Fun to make and handy to carry is this turn-up photo album. Fold a piece of cellophane about $6\frac{1}{2}'' \times 5''$ in half. Tape the ends together with cellophane tape. Attach the transparent pocket near the top of a cardboard divider from your looseleaf book with a strip of tape across the top of the pocket. Turn the pocket up and tape another pocket $\frac{1}{2}''$ below. Continue taping all the way down the pocket page to within $4''$ of the bottom. Then slide your snapshots into the pockets from the side.

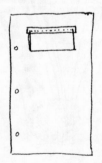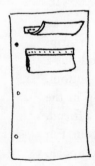

CHAPTER 12

FOR THE RECORD

Spotlight records as the focal point in your room. Combine your own inspirations with some of these versatile ideas for tossing and turning to give your living quarters a touch of the dramatic.

DISC HIDEAWAY

Your 45-rpm discs go incognito when they disappear into a "people" basket. Make this unique container from a large hollow rubber ball that has been discarded. Cut out the top section of the ball, paint on features, glue on sunglasses and use a beret as a lid. Glue on a bow tie to keep the holder firmly balanced.

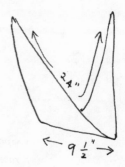

24"

← 9 ½" →

RECORD
CAROUSEL

Serve your 45-rpm records in a whirly carousel. Ideal for browsing, it twirls you the items you want in an instant. Cut several triangles of cloth (height 9½", base 24"). Fold over the triangles to form slings and nail the cloth top and bottom to a foot-high broomstick. Nail the broomstick firmly to a large, flat circle of wood or a tin pie plate. Put a nail through the wood or plate, through several metal washers, and into a sturdy wooden base.

PLATTER PANELS

Tune in on a new wave-length with a backdrop made of pace-setting platter covers. The disc décor makes handsome scenery for your room. Easily mobile, several of these platter panels can be combined to form a room divider. Stitch several clear plastic pockets to a length of canvas or heavy cloth. Insert a wooden coat hanger at the top and install a record album in each pocket. You can hang these panels on doors, or over the edge of your desk. Or you can form a checker-boarded pattern on walls or a folding screen.

BIRD CAGE

If you are lucky enough to have a discarded bird cage, make a carousel for spins and needles. A unique conversation piece, it's a perfect record server. Discs spin around at eye level for you to choose at a glance. Remove the round-the-middle circle of wire from the cage and slide your albums in between each of the bars. Bird-feed holders can store needles or record mitts.

RECORD FILE

Your records are always neat, always ready to go to a party when you file them handily and attractively in soft-drink carrying cartons. Remove the bottle dividers and sort your 45-rpm discs into different cartons. Sparkle-dust the cartons and they will be dressed for any party.

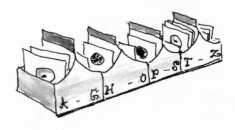

TAKE COVER

Shades of the old wild west protect your record investment when you make this covered wagon. Cut two squares of material large enough to cover the ends of your record holder and round off the corners of the top edges. Cut out a rectangle of cloth large enough to cover the holder from side to side, narrowing it slightly at each end. Stitch all the pieces together, overcasting the edges with wool. Paint on big-spoked wheels and axles and the cover is ready to pioneer against dust and damp on your records.

RECORD
INITIAL

If you're supplying the sound-track for a party with your discs, it's easy to sort out your own records from the other contributions if yours have an identifying mark on the record rim. Before leaving for the party, pile your discs on top of one another. Flick your initial from top to bottom of the stack, using fast-drying nail polish.

In a duet appearance, a waste-basket doubles as a showcase for record covers. Bend several re-painted car license plates into an elongated "Z" shape and hang them over the edges of the wastebasket for records to rest on.

For a really off-beat combo, jazz up your room with a pair of old drums. One nests song music and records, the other holds scraps.

DRUM
SONGS

RECORD WATCHDOG

For maximum protection against scratches and dust, employ a
record watchdog made from two old mittens. Fold the thumbs
inside and stitch the two mittens, palmsides together, about halfway down on both sides. Embroider cloth eyes and a nose, and
add ears. Stitch in a big red felt mouth between the two mittens.
When you place your hand in, puppet-style, your watchdog is
ready to bite the dust off your phonograph records.

CHAPTER 13

FOR YOUR ROOM

Create a stir in your room with some new ingredients for an old recipe. Try a tempting menu of these ideas mixed with your own inspirations to spice an obscure corner or season a neutral nook.

CORNER

BASKET

Do you lack floor space? Then corner a wastebasket. It's never in your way, yet always handy. Cut out one side of a medium-sized cardboard box and tape together the remaining sides to form a triangle. Gift-wrap the basket in glitter paper and it will work overtime brightening a corner.

CARD BOARD

Display birthday cards, hilarious studio cards or unique Christmas cards for more than just the holiday season on the headboard of your bed. Make a slip cover of felt or cloth to slip over your headboard and pin cards in place as an extra special dressing for your room.

HOOP-DEE-DOO

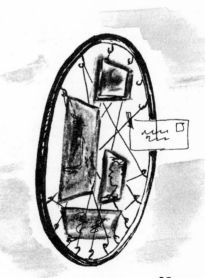

Serve up big helpings of fun from a discarded hula-hoop. Attach several cup hooks around the inside edge of the hoop and stretch lengths of string across in a criss-cross pattern. Pin notes, snapshots and decorations to the string and hang oddments on the hooks. Hang the hoop on the wall of your room and use it as a bulletin board.

PICTURE CORNER

Season a wall with a picture corner to show off your pix without sticky tape marks. Decide which part of a wall you would like for pictures. Then stretch lengths of string vertically from the ceiling moulding to the baseboard. Fasten to one or more strings your photos of movie stars, paintings, music, banners and even pieces of bright, striking paper.

KANGAROO
POUCHES

Dramatic backing for a chair in studio or room, kangaroo pockets hold pens, books and magazines while you read or study, and they simplify perambulating supplies from one room to another. Made from a fold of bright cloth stitched at each end, each pocket is equipped with loops to slip onto a chair back.

CHAIR SLIPPERS

To avoid chair scratches and dents on your bedroom floor, cut out small circles from $\frac{1}{2}''$ thick foam rubber and glue them to the bottom of the legs of your chair. Sprinkle the chair slippers with gold dust for added glitter. Not only will they help prevent holes and marks in your rugs or the floor but they also help make the chair more comfy to sit in.

SPACE MANAGING

If there's standing room only in your room, this lengthy boot will store newspapers, magazines, notes or odds-and-ends. Paint a discarded leaky rainboot or decorate it to resemble a space boot, a sandal or a naked foot. Set it on the floor or hang it on the wall by attaching a piece of wire. You'll find it's an easy shoe to fill.

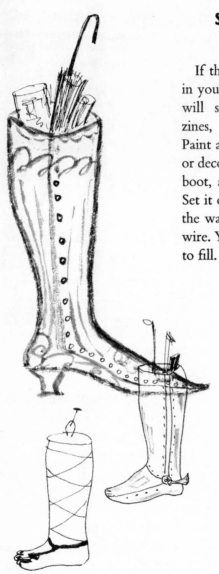

INSIDE

THE CAT'S PAJAMAS

Cut two circles about 15″ in diameter from a piece of heavy cloth, such as corduroy or felt. Cut one circle in half and hem both edges. (Hemming isn't necessary if you use felt.) Cut a piece of contrasting material in the shape of a cat and stitch it on the uncut circle, or draw an outline of a cat and then embroider it. Stitch a Cheshire grin onto the cat's face. Turn the circles inside out, stitch them together all around. Turn the cushion right side out and it's ready to hold pajamas and decorate a bed.

GUM PARKER

Avoid getting extra spice in your gum and gumming up the works with your chewiest wad by parking it at mealtime or bedtime in this handy gum parker. Decorate several small metal aspirin tins with catch-words and phrases and scatter them near bed, books or breakfast nook for fast and non-stick disposal of your current stick of gum.

HANDY DUSTER

To stir the dust from your room here is one hand that doesn't leave fingerprints but instead removes them. Sew an old discarded glove to a piece of soft cloth. Add fingernails cut from red cloth. Cut the gold ring from yellow cloth and sparkle it with a sequin. Keeping your room dustless is a snap with this handy duster.

REMINDER BOARD

Seven ribbons for seven days make a package to mix into a busy schedule. For this handsome reminder board you need a picture frame and a piece of cardboard. Sheathe the cardboard strikingly in taffeta or velvet. Place about seven strips of ribbon diagonally across the velvet and tack them at each edge. Fit the beribboned velvet into a picture frame to hold postcards, invitations, letters, photos and memos. The occasional gold button suspends a pen or pencil.

HIDEAWAY HAMPER

This brainy-looking individual sits on your bed as a mock pillow and cleverly hides your hand-laundry items. Stitch him up from two circles of stiff, heavy cloth of whatever size you wish, leaving an opening at the top for laundry. Attach a beanie to one side of the opening to form a hinged lid. Add wool hair, ears, a mouth and black spectacles. You might line him with cardboard so he'll hold his shape when empty.

SMILING
LAUNDRY BAG

Keep your room as neat as a pin with a smiling laundry bag. Cut two pieces of cotton or felt in the shape shown, about $15\frac{1}{2}''$ wide and $21''$ long. On one piece sew bangs made from black or yellow cotton across the top. Add eyelashes and red lips. Then stitch the two sides together. Attach it to a clothes hanger with clothespins.

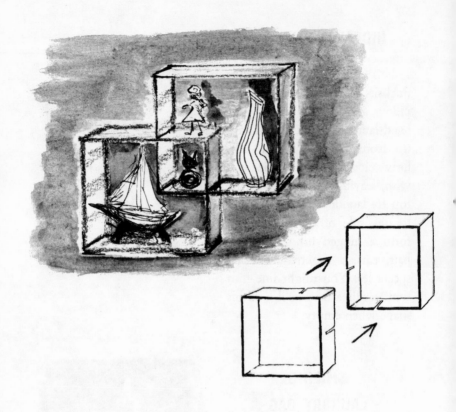

SHADOW BOXING

Display your trophies and ornaments in these modern shadow boxes. Cut two 3″ slices from a corrugated cardboard box about 9″ square. On two sides of each frame, cut a slit 1½″ deep exactly in the middle of the side. Place the slits of one square over the slits of the other. Press together. Tape the outside edges and paint the frames attractively.

A STUFFED SHIRT FOR YOUR PJ'S

Here's a stuffed shirt that looks hilarious on your bed and serves as a cushion as well as a pajama holder. Find one of Dad's discarded shirts and cut off the arms and the shirttails. Stitch across the bottom and the armholes so that the shirt forms a bag. Undo the buttons to insert the pajamas, then dress up your stuffed shirt with a smart bow tie.

SLIPPER GRIPPER

To make a setting place for your slippers, cut a piece of cardboard into an oval about 20″×9″. Cut four thin ovals 5″ long. Staple two of them halfway down the large oval to form arms, the other two at the bottom as feet. Paint on a face and add wool hair. Make a pair of pants of half an oval of cloth and staple them around the edge, leaving a pocket for your slippers. Tack the feet to a wooden stand and rest the gripper against your bed.

VASE TRIO

Grace a shelf with this delicate vase to hold a trio of flowers. Criss-cross three plastic or glass toothbrush containers to form a 3-legged support and glue them together about halfway down. Decorate the holder with shells or decals. Partly fill with water and add a flower or two or three.

Let six small jars of uniform size help you keep your premises tidy. Cut a piece of one-inch board into a hexagon, each side about two inches long. To each side nail a jar lid. Nail the pinwheel to your bulletin board or closet door with a large nail. Fill jars with odds and ends such as safety pins, tacks, string and sewing supplies and screw a jar into each lid. When you want a particular item, just spin the wheel.

TIDY-UP PINWHEEL

HANGER

SPACER

Clothes in your closet won't be wrinkled and crushed if you have a hanger spacer. Use a heavy cardboard strip about 3″ wide and as long as the clothes rack. Cut slits about $\frac{1}{2}$″ wide at intervals of an inch. Wrap the cardboard over the rack with the slits on top and tape it into place.

CHAPTER 14

SCHOOL SCOOPS

Scoop next term's schoolwork ahead of dead-line with a handful of handy gadgets to help with homework.

NOTE SACK

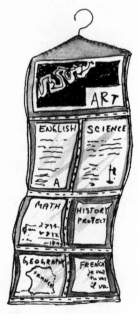

Practical and convenient, a note sack operates as a see-through vertical drawer. Stitch a length of heavy cloth firmly to a wire hanger and staple or stitch on plastic bags as pockets. Insert note-books on each subject in a different section and you will find them speedily. Your notes are always ready for take-off to anywhere you want to work, yet can be hung out of the way in a closet.

FOR POSTERS

You can create posters for school elections, displays, etc., in a jiffy with mucilage bottles filled with poster paints. Outline the letters in pencil and then, using a ruler, draw the letters with the mucilage bottles. You will get even, clean-cut lines more than $\frac{1}{4}''$ wide with no brush or felt fuzz.

BOOK EASEL

To simplify homework set up your textbooks or notebooks on a book easel. Make it from a piece of cardboard $12\frac{1}{2}'' \times 25''$. Fold a rectangle $9''$ from one end and $7''$ from the other end and glue the two ends together to form a wedge. Tape on a $7'' \times 1''$ ledge to hold books in place.

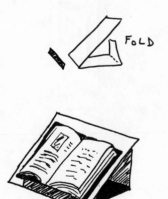

97

LEAVE YOUR MARK

Turn school items into decorative grace notes in your room or display prize essays and 100% exams by tacking them in transparent plastic bags to a door or room divider. Add a bright border of felt or paper to identify the subject and give the divider a dramatic effect.

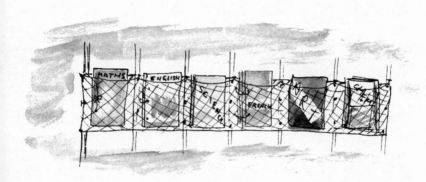

NETTED NOTES

Try an aerial defense against notebook clutter with a network of neat notes. Visibility: good. Location: easy. Hang a length of 24″-wide net folded double along a wall in attic or storeroom and tack it into place every foot or so. At the end of each term, store away your notes according to subject and you will avoid wasting time burrowing through boxes for the papers you want.

NOTE CARTING

Notes can go mobile filed in an old wire grocery cart. Paint the perambulating storehouse and insert dividers to aid filing.

HONEYCOMB UNIT

If your notebooks can be rolled up, they can repose in a honeycomb unit. Round cereal cartons glued in vari-shaped clusters will fit any space available. Alphabetically classified notebooks slide easily into the molecular holder for safekeeping.

PROJECT CARRIER

A special carrier facilitates delivery of awkward art projects or maps from home to school. Make this handy caddy by gluing empty wax-paper tubes together and tape on a ribbon for carrying. Rolled-up posters, drawings and maps will arrive in A-1 condition.

TYPEWRITER COVER

Inside information to help you brew up term papers or letters is the new interior décor for your typewriter cover. Cut a square of cardboard to fit inside the cover. Using sturdy cloth, stitch on pockets for envelopes, paper, typewriter eraser, pencils, type cleaner brush, tape, stamps, etc., and tape in place.

LOCKER

TOTEBAG

A handy totebag catchall will keep things from falling out of an overstuffed locker. The totebag can be made from a plastic dry-cleaning bag. Stitch on seam binding to divide into pockets, insert a hanger and install in your locker for books, gloves and locker overflow.

CHAPTER 15

SEWING AIDS

*As gifts for others or as gifts for yourself,
here are some witty wraps to keep you in
stitches from hand to toe.*

SPOOL SPACE

This thread dispenser will put an end to knots and tangles in
your sewing box. Find a box about $1\frac{3}{4}''$ high, $2\frac{1}{2}''$ wide and as long
as possible. Opposite each spool of thread make slits about $\frac{3}{4}''$ deep.
Pull the thread out through each slit and put the box cover back
on. Always leave a bit of the thread ends hanging out of the box
ready for use.

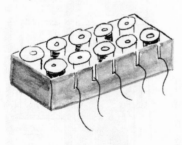

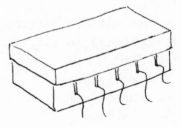

SEWING
ENSEMBLE

Sewing supplies are always within reach on this handy board. Nail a piece of wood 3 feet × 3 inches at right angles to a piece of pegboard 3 feet wide and 2 feet high, to form a shelf. Stick nails or pegs into the perforations and hang up scissors, thread, tape, etc. Use the shelf to hold patterns and other sewing supplies.

A
SEW-AND-SEW

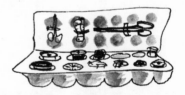

This compartmented sewing kit started life as an egg box. Brighten it up with a coat of paint and attach a pin cushion to the lid for pins and needles. A flock of spools fits into the compartments and scissors can be taped on the lid or kept inside.

GLOVE KIT

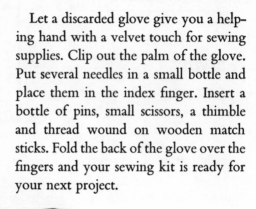

Let a discarded glove give you a helping hand with a velvet touch for sewing supplies. Clip out the palm of the glove. Put several needles in a small bottle and place them in the index finger. Insert a bottle of pins, small scissors, a thimble and thread wound on wooden match sticks. Fold the back of the glove over the fingers and your sewing kit is ready for your next project.

SEWING SLIPPER

Sewing items repose in slippered ease in this holder. Cover a discarded slipper with a bright remnant. Insert your sewing tape to pull through the open toe. Add spools of thread, thimble, scissors, etc. For gem-like glitter, sew sequins and beads to the slipper in a flower design.

KNITTING

KIT

Knitting needles of a feather flock together in this holder. Cut a length of corrugated cardboard from an old carton. Make it the length of your longest knitting needle and as wide as needed for the number of needles. Roll it up in a tube and tape it in position. Cover it with gift paper or paint it and insert your knitting needles.

JIFFY PINCUSHION

Make a pincushion in a jiffy from an old adhesive tape spool. Remove the spool from the rim and stick a piece of tape across the hole in the middle. Place a wad of cotton batting on top of the spool, place a piece of cloth over the top, and set it into the outer rim in position. Clip off any extra cloth hanging out of the bottom.

PIN CARRIER

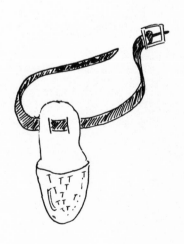

Do you have to look all over for pins when you sew? Keep them at your elbow and avoid spills with this clever pin carrier. Cut away the rubber toe and part of the sole of a worn-out rubber. Cut two slits in the sole about an inch long and two inches apart and slide a belt through them. Fill the toe with pins. At your next sewing session buckle on your pins and you're set for action.

106

CHAPTER 16

SPORTIN' LIFE

Roll up your score with a few striking ideas for sports equipment.

BALL PARK

Make a "whole in one" with the accumulation of balls around your house. Park them all—everything from table tennis to golf balls—in a large worn-out basketball or football. Carve off a section of the top to form a hinged lid and glue a table tennis ball to it as a picker-upper. Paint or varnish the ball and sit it, trophy-like, on a shelf in your room.

RACKET PACK

A racket holder keeps your badminton or tennis racket safely out of the way and protects it from scratches. Cut off a small section of casing from an old worn-out car tire. Near the outside edges snip two small "V's" for the racket to rest in. Nail the holder to a basement or garage wall.

FOR THE BIRDS

Keep track of your badminton birds or tennis balls with this piggy-back racket cover. Cut a piece of cloth large enough to go around your badminton or tennis racket. Stitch a rectangular pocket to the top side of the cover.

Fold the cover over and stitch around two sides. Thread a drawstring through the bottom side. The racket cover not only holds birds or balls but also keeps your racket in A-1 shape.

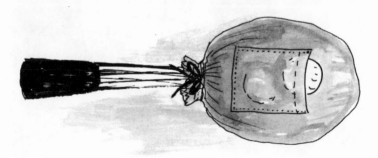

Table tennis balls are always ready to pong into action when you store them in a convenient ejector-dispenser. Roll a length of cardboard to a diameter slightly smaller than a wax-paper tube. About two inches from one end cut out a circle the size of a ball. Tape up the roll and glue small paper cups in place to seal the ends. Slide the roll inside a wax-paper tube and insert balls through the opening. At table tennis time, it will be fun to slide the tube open and bounce out a ball.

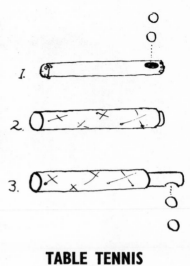

**TABLE TENNIS
BALL DISPENSER**

SADDLE SAVER

Protect your bicycle seat from rainy weather with this jiffy cover. Find a plastic bag large enough to fit over the saddle. Should it begin to rain when you're out, you can quickly tie on the cover with a shoelace or a string before parking your bike.

FOOTFALL

That yardline moves closer into your room when you let your foot fall on a football mat. Cut out a giant football from an old gunny sack. Bind all around the edges with heavy string and embroider or stitch on the football lacings with dark colored twine. Stitch on stripes of material for your team's colors, and also their pennant and name. A footfall underfoot will decorate your floor and keep your bare feet from chill.

FOOTPRINT IN THE SAND

Make a big splash at the beach with this unusual footprint in the sand. First cut out a paper pattern for a very large foot—at least 5 feet long by $2\frac{1}{2}$ feet wide. Then use the pattern to cut a giant foot out of burlap. Cut another footprint of the same size out of terry cloth and stitch it to the burlap. Add a pocket for suntan lotion and stitch on red cloth toenails.

SPORT SHORTS

You can make an ideal picnic and beach carryall for fun supplies from an old pair of shorts. Stitch the bottoms of the legs together and then attach a large pocket on each side to hold hair spray, towels, books, etc. String a belt through the belt loops to carry it. Once at the beach, you can remove the contents and use the totebag as a seat.

CHAPTER 17

TELEPHONE-ITIS

*Ring around the dial and take the sting out of
the ring of Mr. Bell's bell.*

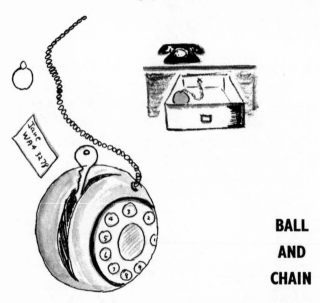

BALL
AND
CHAIN

Chain phone numbers to the phone table and encircle valuable
items in this unique storehouse. Slit a hollow rubber ball with
scissors, squeeze it open to insert precious phone numbers, memos,
keys, coins, etc. Snap the ball shut and staple one end of a chain to
the ball, the other end of the chain to the inside of your telephone
desk drawer. Paint on a phone dial featuring your phone number.
Even in a cluttered drawer the ball will always be easy to find.

NUMBER PLEASE

You won't lose your friends' phone numbers if you make this clever twirl-and-dial number wheel. Write your friends' names, addresses and phone numbers on cards $1\frac{3}{4}'' \times 3''$ and punch two holes near the top of each card. Bend a sturdy piece of wire into a $3\frac{1}{2}''$ square and string on the cards in alphabetical order. Bend the bottom of the wire square to hook on your telephone or sit on your desk.

MESSAGE
TAKER

If your family practically runs an answer-phone service for you when you're out, they'll appreciate this handy message taker. Use a cigar box or a box made of heavy cardboard. Put a note pad and a pencil inside. Glue a cardboard clockface on top and tack on two hands. Set the hands for the time you expect to return each time you leave. Your family will be able to tell callers the best time to call back again.

HOLD UP

Why increase wear and tear on a telephone cord by leaving the receiver dangling while you go to find someone? A slim section from a discarded bicycle tire casing makes a convenient holder. Paint it and tack it up beside the phone or attach it to a pad on the phone table.

TELEPHONE
TIME

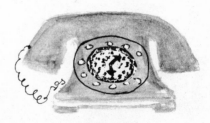

Are you conversation-happy? Do your LP talks force the family to a busy signal every time there's a phone call for you? Try taping time to the phone. Tape or glue an old watch to the middle of the telephone dial to keep you posted on how the time flies when you talk!

CHAPTER 18

TRAVEL

Here are your passport and visas for home or highway travel fun.

For a world of difference in your room, a wastebasket, encircled by a map of the world, converts into a handy headquarters for vacation planning. It holds brochures, travel folders, maps and booklets ready for plotting your itinerary. Coat the basket with plastic spray to preserve the surface. Pin or clip on postcards, matchcovers or photos of places you've visited.

VACATION

PLANNER

HANG UP YOUR HOLIDAY

As a souvenir of shifting scenery, hang up your holiday after it's over in the form of these decorative maps. Cut out each state or country you visit from a large travel map that you can get at any service station. Glue the maps onto cardboard backing, spray with varnish, then thread them onto a decorative string and stretch them across your room.

CUSHION IN MOTION

This cushion will help you tote glasses and notebooks and keep you comfortable wherever you go. Cut a 30″ × 12″ rectangle of cloth. Fold up 6″ on the outside to make a pocket and stitch it up the middle to form two compartments. Fold the cloth double and stitch around three sides. Fill the cushion with stuffing or discarded nylons and stitch up the fourth side. Attach a handle made from the same cloth.

PURSE-SIZE TRAVEL PACK

Sightseeing or site sewing, a purse-size travel pack holds sewing supplies ready for emergency repairs. Thoroughly remove all the lipstick from a handsome lipstick tube. Insert a puff of cotton batting to pincushion needles and pins. Wind a vari-colored thread supply onto toothpicks or long thin bobbins.

TRAVELLER'S SNAP ALBUM

Cover the snapshots of your jubilant jaunt with the leather case that held the travellers' checks. Trim photos to the right size, punch two holes in the edge about $1\frac{5}{8}''$ apart and install them on the clips in the case.

SUNTAN KIT

A minute-size medicine cabinet for migrators is stocked with pills, mosquito and suntan lotion, sunglasses and mirror. Make it from a fairly large circle of terry cloth to which you stitch several contrasting patch pockets opening on the edge of the circle. Run a drawstring around the circumference. Closed, it's a handbag—ideal for travel. Open, it's a beach seat—perfect for suntanning.

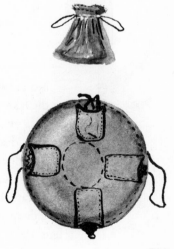

CHAPTER 19

GRAB BAG

A whole parade of items to dispense with problems around the house.

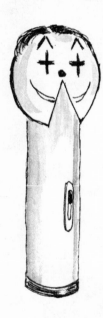

FLASHLIGHT

PROTECTOR

No clowning around will harm a flashlight at the lake or at home when the lens is shielded with a spongy protector. Cut a slim wedge from a discarded tennis or rubber ball. Make this wedge just large enough for the ball to fit tightly over the lens end of the flashlight. Decorate the cover and install the light. Should you drop your flashlight, you won't smash the lens glass.

TOOTHPASTE
DISPENSER

Be on the bandwagon with an automatic toothpaste dispenser. Take a large metal clip, paint it and clip it over the bottom end of the toothpaste tube. Hang it on the wall. To dispense toothpaste, simply press the tube against the wall. No more mess and no more accidents from falling toothpaste tubes.

SHAMPOO GOGGLES

Shampoo perfect, these co-operative leak-proof goggles keep the soap out of your eyes. Carefully remove the lenses from a pair of old sunglasses. Cellophane tape in clear celluloid lenses. Cut a piece of terry cloth 19″×4″, stitch it into a long tube and stuff with cotton batting. Stitch the tubing firmly all around the glasses with stitches right through the celluloid lenses. Thin the cotton batting for the section over the bridge of the nose. With these goggles hair washing is a cinch.

FIRST-AID KIT

There's a single-file procession of emergency supplies in this practical first-aid kit. Glue together, side to side, three plastic turnstick tubes that shaving lotion and stick cologne are sold in. Fill the first tube with band-aids, the second tube with cotton batting and the third with strips of gauze. A flick of the wrist turns up whatever you need in an instant.

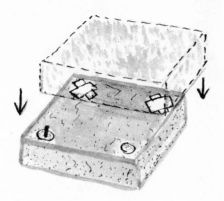

CAR WASHER

Shine up the family car to a pace-setting sparkle in half the usual time with a car washer. Cut indentations in each of the four corners of a regular car sponge. Stitch tiny magnets inside each hole and stitch another sponge on top. The magnets keep all parts of the sponge on the car all the time you wipe or polish. You finish fast when every stroke counts.

INDEX